The Hunt

based on the film Jagten *by*
THOMAS VINTERBERG
and
TOBIAS LINDHOLM

adapted for the stage by
DAVID FARR

FABER & FABER

First published in 2019
by Faber and Faber Limited
74–77 Great Russell Street, London WC1B 3DA

Typeset by Country Setting, Kingsdown, Kent CT14 8ES
Printed in England by CPI Group (UK) Ltd, Croydon CR0 4YY

Copyright in the original film *Jagten*
© Thomas Vinterberg and Tobias Lindholm 2012

A CIP record for this book
is available from the British Library

ISBN 978-0-571-35437-5

2 4 6 8 10 9 7 5 3 1

The Hunt in this stage adaptation was first performed at the Almeida Theatre, London, on 17 June 2019. The cast, in alphabetical order, was as follows:

Hilde Michele Austin
Marcus Stuart Campbell
Rune Adrian Der Gregorian
Ragner Keith Higham
Gunner Danny Kirrane
Lucas Tobias Menzies
Mikala Poppy Miller
Tomas Itoya Osagiede
Theo Justin Salinger
Palme Jethro Skinner
Per / Pastor Howard Ward
Clara Abbiegail Mills / Taya Tower / Florence White
Peter Harrison Houghton / George Nearn Stuart

Direction Rupert Goold
Design Es Devlin
Costume Evie Gurney
Light Neil Austin
Sound and Composition Adam Cork
Movement Botis Seva
Casting Amy Ball CDG
Children's Casting Verity Naughton

Characters

Hilde
fifty-five years old, head of the infants' school

Lucas
forty years old, teacher in the infants' school

Clara
six years old

Peter
six years old

Gunner
thirty-nine years old, Peter's father

Mikala
thirty-nine years old, Clara's mother

Theo
forty years old, Clara's father

Rune
forty years old

Per
sixty years old, child protection officer

Marcus
sixteen years old, Lucas's son

and

Pastor
fifty-five years old

Ragnar, Tomas, Palme, Anders
of the lodge

Children
from the school

THE HUNT

Act One

An infants' school. Northern Denmark. October.
  Hilde is speaking to us. Lucas is there.

Hilde Welcome, everyone. It's lovely to see so many
familiar faces.

The children are just getting ready. I hope you got here
OK despite the winds. I hear there are trees down all
along the edge of the forest so please do be careful on
your way home.

As you know we at the infants' school have always
enjoyed the harvest festival, something to really cheer us
up as the nights turn darker. I think this year's is going
to be the best ever.

I want to thank all you parents for bringing in the
produce and for helping with your children's costumes.

I want to thank Rune Skillig for the lend of the van
and Tilly Mordahl for the lovely hanging fruit and
vegetables. Thank you, Tilly.

I want to thank one person especially. Our newest
teacher Lucas Bruun has worked very hard with the
children to make this spectacle for you today. Thank
you, Lucas.

Finally I want to say as someone who has run the
school for more than ten years.

We are a small community. The happiness of our
children is everything. Our hopes and dreams rest in
these tiny souls. And to spend each day with them is
a kind of heaven.

Shall we begin?

SCENE TWO

Eight naked men – the Men of the Lodge. Soaking wet.
Approaching the jetty of a river. Freezing cold air. They
sing. It gets faster and faster.

Men
Oh eight men they go swimming
In the water oh so cold
But when the first man's jumping
In the water oh so cold
He cries out I am dying
In the water oh so cold
So the second man he goes jumping
In the water oh so cold
Then the third man saves the second man
From the water oh so cold
And the fourth man saves the third man
From the water oh so cold
The fifth man saves the fourth man
From the water oh so cold
And the sixth man saves the fifth man
From the water oh so cold
Then the seventh man saves the sixth man
From the water oh so cold
And the eighth man saves the seventh man
From the water oh so cold.

But the eighth man is the last man
In the water oh so cold.
And no one saves the last man
From the water oh so cold.
So if you want to know
The moral of this song
Don't be the last man
In the water oh so cold!

As the song finishes we see Clara, a six-year-old girl.
She is quietly and intensely wrapping a small parcel.

SCENE THREE

The clock says Friday 15 November, 3.02 p.m.
A classroom in an infants' school. About eighteen tiny
chairs around modern tables.
Lucas Bruun is tidying the classroom which is chaotic,
with plasticine and torn-up paper everywhere.
He is on the phone. He speaks quietly, staying calm.

Lucas No listen. Talk to him . . . Just listen to what he
has to say . . . Susanna, please.

I know what the courts said but the 'arrangement'
isn't working. You've moved him eighty miles away. He
misses me.

I didn't say that . . . I didn't say that he prefers being
with me. I just said he misses me.

Please don't shout. You always do this . . . You
escalate, your voice starts to go higher . . .

How can my staying calm make you explode? . . . It's
not easy for me. I'm the one who doesn't see him . . .
Susanna . . .

She has put the phone down. He stands there. He
stares at the room.
Enter Hilde.

Hilde I thought maybe you'd gone.

Lucas Just clearing up.

Hilde Can I ask you a favour?

Lucas Sure.

Hilde Two parents are late picking up.

Lucas No problem.

Hilde I know it's my turn but I have to write the health and safety report tonight. I don't suppose the parents will be long . . .

Lucas Hilde, it's fine. I'm only going home anyway.

Hilde Friday night? Nothing planned?

Lucas Just one hungry dog to feed.

She looks at the room.

Hilde What happened here?

Lucas Ah yes. A slight battle broke out.

Hilde Lucas . . .

Lucas It was the final twenty minutes. It's the weekend. They needed some fun. I know. I'm a soft touch.

Hilde You have plasticine in your hair.

Lucas Which two children have been left behind?

Hilde Peter Jensen. His mother is ill in bed, so Gunner is driving over from the office. You know Gunner, don't you?

Lucas Who doesn't know Gunner?

Hilde A larger-than-life character.

Lucas Rule 1. Never drink beer with Gunner. Rule 2. I shouldn't have drunk beer with Gunner. Who's the other child?

Hilde Take a guess.

Lucas Clara Kallstrom.

Hilde I don't know how many times I've warned them.

Lucas What is it this time?

Hilde Apparently Mikala thought Theo was picking her up, Theo thought Mikala was picking her up, now Theo is in no state to get in a car, and Mikala's rushing here from work like a rally driver.

Lucas Mikala doesn't work Fridays.

Hilde She works at the logging company.

Lucas But not Fridays. She has an art class Friday morning.

Hilde You're Theo's friend. Please talk to him. We can't keep doing this.

Lucas Hilde. You have make-up on.

Hilde Maybe a little.

Lucas You always wear lipstick to complete the health and safety report?

Hilde All right. I do have to do the report first. But the truth is I have a date. Just a coffee date. Not a real date. Coffee and cake.

Lucas Is he handsome?

Hilde He's a man. That's all the qualification he needs.

Beat.

How about you? Anyone new?

Lucas Not at the moment.

Hilde Something wrong with the women in this town? You wouldn't be short of offers. After the harvest festival I had written applications. You can't hide forever you know.

Lucas Just get the kids, Hilde.

Hilde You're an angel.

She kisses him, leaving a little lipstick on his cheek.

Hilde If you need me I'll be in the office. Finishing the –

Lucas Health and safety report.

She leaves. Lucas stares. Checks his phone. Calls.

Marcus, it's your dad here. Call me, please. I know your mother doesn't want you ringing me but I . . .

Enter Clara. Six years old. She stares at him.
There is a quiet intensity to her.

I'll try you again later.

He hangs up.

Hey, Clara. Come in. Your parents are late, yes?

Clara I think they forgot me.

Lucas No, they didn't forget. They just got delayed. Your mum's coming now. Where's Peter?

Clara He's . . .

Lucas Yes?

Clara He's having a . . . He's going for a . . .

She whispers in his ear.

Lucas Well, that's nothing to whisper about. We all need to do that sometimes. Don't we?

She nods.

Come and help me clear up this mess we made. You don't like mess, do you? So shall we get rid of it? You do that side. I'll do this side. OK?

They begin.

What are you doing this weekend? Do you know?

She shakes her head.

I think your dad and I might be going hunting together. Although he's such a lousy shot I'm worried he might shoot me by mistake.

She drops what she's carrying.

I didn't mean that. That was a joke. OK?

She nods. A small intense moment.
Enter Peter loudly. Shorts down to his ankles.

Peter Lucas! I'm still here!

Lucas So it would appear.

Peter I need you to wipe my bottom.

Lucas You can't do it yourself?

Peter No.

Lucas All right, I'm coming. Clara – keep up the good work. (*To Peter.*) You know it really might be time to learn to do that on your own.

He walks out. Clara stands alone. She tidies the chairs slowly until they are in perfect order. There is something very particular about this.
Then Lucas walks back in.

Lucas Well now. That's a good job you've done.

Clara Did you wash your hands?

Lucas Yes, I did.

Beat. Peter runs in.

Peter Can we play a game while we wait?

Lucas Criminals don't get to play games.

Peter I'm not a criminal.

Lucas I saw you squash that fly before break.

Peter Only because it was annoying me.

Lucas And if you annoy me, should I squash you? Hmm?

Peter No.

Lucas Because it so happens I'm in a squashing mood.

He suddenly chases him, grabs him, squeezes him tight. Peter screams in delight. He fights Lucas, who suddenly fakes death.

No you're too strong! I can't breathe. Can't breathe!

Lucas appears to collapse and lies flat. Clara watches, worried.

Peter You're not dead! You're lying. Lucas, wake up!

Lucas is still. Clara looks deeply worried.

Clara Lucas? Lucas!

Beat. She rushes forward. Then Lucas rises.

Lucas He lives.

He chases Peter, who knocks over all the chairs again. Clara watches.
Then Lucas's phone rings. He sees who it is.

Marcus? Yeah. Hi. Hi. No it's a good time. Wait a moment. Kids, stay here. I won't be long.

He leaves.

Peter It's really quiet. It's weird how quiet it is. I've never stayed late before. Have you stayed late before?

Clara I can't remember.

Peter Who's picking you up? My dad's coming in the big car. Its seats are leather.

Clara Did you see? Lucas has lipstick on his face.

Peter Where?

Clara On his left cheek.

Peter Maybe it's his girlfriend.

Clara He doesn't have a girlfriend. He only lives with Max.

Peter Who's Max?

Clara He's a labrador. And he doesn't wear lipstick.

Peter looks around. Whispers.

Peter Hey. You want to see something?

She nods. He reaches into his small satchel. He brings out a phone.

Clara Whose is that?

Peter It's mine. It was my dad's but now he's got a new one so.

He turns it on. Is about to show Clara something.

Promise to tell no one. I mean *no one*?

Pause. She nods. He shows her.

I found this video on it.

Clara What is it?

Peter It's a woman, stupid.

Clara What's she doing?

Beat.

Peter Her skin is shiny.

They stare at the phone.

Clara Why is it on your phone?

Peter I don't know. Dad said everything was deleted but I found it in the history.

Clara Does your dad know her?

Peter No! Of course not! He wouldn't know a woman like that.

Clara Then why is she on his phone?

Peter Look. That's a man.

Beat.

Clara What's that?

Peter That's his thing.

Clara What thing?

Peter You know.

He whispers. Pause. They stare.

Clara Why is it pointing up?

Peter It's like a rod.

They watch. A quiet and very intense moment.

SCENE FOUR

*Peter and Clara are now sitting apart. No phone in sight.
Lucas enters with Gunner.*

Gunner Of course you have to come!

Lucas Maybe.

Gunner No maybes. It's what we do every year at Advent! The hunting, the drinking and then . . . Armageddon.

Peter Daddy!

Gunner Ah, here he is. The heir to the throne. Eh?

Peter Where's Mum?

Gunner She's at home.

Peter Why is she at home?

Gunner She's sick. Apparently. And anyway I wanted to pick you up myself!

He hugs him. Clara watches.

How has he been?

Lucas He's been very good.

Gunner I doubt that. Get your shoes on, soldier. Take the keys and you can let yourself in.

Peter Can I turn on the radio?

Gunner Just this once. Watch that leather! You're paying for every scratch.

Peter Bye, Lucas!

Lucas See you on Monday.

Exit Peter.

Gunner So are you coming tomorrow or not?

Lucas Why not?

Gunner Good man. No point playing the recluse. Show her you're thriving without her. You must bring Marcus.

Lucas Marcus isn't here at the moment.

Gunner I don't know why you stand for it.

Lucas I don't 'stand' for it. The courts ruled . . .

Gunner Fuck the courts. Show her who's boss!

Lucas Gunner. Language.

He gestures to the listening Clara.

Gunner Marcus is nearly sixteen. Right?

Lucas In January.

Gunner So we need to initiate him. Every sixteen-year-old gets their initiation.

Lucas We may have to delay it a little. Until the spring maybe.

Gunner Listen. The best shot in the town has a son, I want him in my lodge. Just because he's moved away with the crazy woman . . . Marcus is family. Get him up here tomorrow. Don't take no for an answer.

Lucas I'll try.

Gunner notices the lipstick.

Gunner What's this? Been at the ladies again?

Lucas What? Oh . . .

He wipes his lipstick.

Oh that was . . .

Gunner You devil.

Lucas No, it was just Hilde . . .

Gunner Hilde!

Lucas No, not like that . . .

Gunner It all becomes clear. The quiet man. Questions will be asked tomorrow night, my friend. The lodge will require answers!

The sound of a horn.

Better go before he destroys that car.

Gunner leaves.

Pause. Lucas looks at Clara.

Lucas So. It's just you and me.

Beat.

Shimmy up there. We've got some time before your mum gets here.

He smiles at her.

You know I remember when you were a baby. In your mum and dad's house. I held you in my arms. You were sick on my suit. But since I started working here, these last few months I feel I've got to know you.
 And you know what I think?

Clara No.

Lucas I think there are a lot of things in your head that you don't say. Peter there, he says things before he's thought them. But you keep it all in. I can be a bit like that too, so I understand. And I know it can be hard, in a schoolroom or in a . . . noisy house, to make yourself heard. But I want you to try and say a little more what you think. What you feel. Hmm? Will you try?

Clara Who were you talking to on the phone?

Lucas My son.

Clara Marcus.

Lucas Do you remember him?

Clara Dad says you're sad because you can't see him any more.

Lucas Does he . . .

Clara Because Marcus lives in the city.

Lucas Yes, he does.

Clara And so you're very sad.

Beat.
    She gets up, walks to her drawer.
    Then she takes out the present. Wrapped.

Lucas What is this?

He unwraps it. It's the bright red heart-shaped lollipop.

Is this for me?

She suddenly hugs him.
    Then, though we do not see it clearly, it seems that she kisses him on the lips. The kiss lingers for just a little longer than it should before Lucas moves back. Pause of deep shock.

Clara, listen. I can't accept this. You should give it to a friend.
    And that kind of kiss? It's for mummies and daddies. It's not for teachers. OK?
    You should take this back.

He holds out the lollipop. Beat. There is a buzz.

Clara It's not from me.

Lucas (*gently*) You just gave it to me.

Clara It's not from me.

Lucas It's OK. Nothing's wrong. But you should take it back.

Clara suddenly runs out.

Clara, come back.

Beat. Mikala enters. Very stressed.

Mikala Oh man, I'm so late. How are you, handsome?

Lucas quickly puts a red heart-shaped lollipop down on the desk.

The bloody car's all fucked up, it never starts in the cold. Theo was supposed to be doing the pick-up, I told him. Where is Clara?

Lucas She's . . . hidden herself.

Mikala You're playing hide-and-seek?

Lucas You know you and Theo need to sort this out. It's the third time this week you're late. On Tuesday morning I found Clara walking to school on her own, which isn't safe.

Mikala Jesus Christ, you really are the schoolteacher.

Lucas You know she can't step on the cracks. Which means she doesn't look where she's going.

Mikala You lecturing me on my own child?

Lucas Where were you anyway?

Mikala It's none of your business where I was. If Theo hadn't forgotten the one thing I asked him to do . . . He's drunk half the time. Can't hold down a job. And now he's finding it hard to keep his prick up so . . .

Lucas I don't need to know that. Just be on time. OK?

Mikala Sorry, Lucas. You have such high expectations of us. And we always let you down.

Lucas I'll find Clara.

He makes to leave.

Mikala Do you really like it here? In this shitty little room? Talking to six-year-olds all day.

Lucas Why shouldn't I?

Mikala But after teaching at the secondary school. Doesn't it kill you?

Lucas The secondary school closed.

Mikala So move to the city . . .

Lucas I don't want to move to the city.

Mikala Because the bitch is there?

Lucas Susanna is not a bitch.

Mikala Don't you go mad here? In that house? No one for miles.

Beat.

Talking to you is like scaling a fucking castle wall. You know that?

Clara enters. Mikala does not see her.

But the thing about castles. We all want to know what's inside.

She is close to him. Clara stares.
There is something incredibly cold about this glare.
There is another buzz.

Lucas I'll get it.

He walks out.
Mikala turns. Goes to Clara, hugs her hard. Kisses her. Clara avoids her kiss.

Mikala Hey baby. What's wrong?

Clara Nothing.

Mikala Well, shall we go? I have to pick up some food on the way. There's nothing in the house again. What would you like? Hmm? Anything you want? Anything at all.

Clara is looking at the heart-shaped lollipop. Mikala sees.

What you looking at?

Mikala picks up the lollipop.

Clara Don't touch it.

Mikala Is it yours?

Clara Lucas tried to give it to me.
But I don't want it.

Mikala You love lollipops.

Clara I don't want it.

Enter Theo and Lucas. Theo is smoking.

Lucas Theo is here.

Mikala What are you doing here?

Mikala puts the heart down.

Theo You asking me that? I got a fucking SOS. Child abandoned alone in schoolroom.

Lucas Theo, you can't smoke in here.

Theo does not put out the cigarette.

Mikala I'm the one who got the SOS. I was told you couldn't drive.

Theo I was told you couldn't come.

Lucas Theo, you can't . . .

Mikala I was told I had to come! Despite me making it crystal bloody clear that it was your turn to pick up.

Lucas Theo!

Theo I have no memory of that.

Mikala Well that's a surprise. You remember who I am, do you?

Theo (*putting out cigarette*) I remember you don't work Fridays.

Mikala I was busy! I told you this morning. I couldn't have made it clearer! Did you drive here?

Theo I had one beer for lunch.

Mikala And how big was that one beer?

Theo What difference does it make?

Mikala We'll talk about that when we're home. Clara, come on, baby. Let's just hope the car starts.

Theo I've got the truck. She loves the truck. Don't you, Clara?

Mikala You're not taking her in the truck.

Theo Why not?

Mikala Because there's too many trees between here and home for you to wrap yourself around. Next time stay sober or live in a less forested environment. Clara, you get in Mummy's car. OK?

Theo I've had one beer!

Mikala Why does this happen every time!? I ask you to do one thing! Did you clear that gun from the kitchen?

Theo I will when I get back.

Mikala He leaves it in the kitchen! Like it's a dustpan.

Theo You never know who might break in.

Mikala I'd welcome them in, open arms. They might cook a meal once in a while. Clara, get your coat and bag, I'll see you outside. Lucas, thanks for waiting for the mad couple.

She walks out. Clara gets her bag.

Theo Clara baby, get your coat on, do as your mother says.

Clara Is Mummy angry with you?

Theo No no. She just wants to chop my head off, that's all. (*To Lucas, quietly.*) Lucas, my man. We going hunting tomorrow?

Lucas Yes, I think so.

Theo And you're staying for the drinking this time? No sneaking off.

Lucas That's if you're allowed out at all.

Theo Oh that? That's just foreplay.

He laughs. Beat.

You go with your mother, Clara. Race you home.

Lucas Don't drive too fast.

Theo Grand fucking Prix.

He leaves. Clara does up her coat.

Lucas Clara. Listen.

He sees Theo has left behind his cigarettes.

Theo?!

He walks out.
    Clara gets her bag. She stands alone. She walks to the lollipop. Stares at it. Hilde enters. In her coat. Ready for her date.

Hilde You still here, Clara? I'm locking up now. I thought your parents were here.

Beat.

Clara? Are you OK?

Beat.

Clara I hate Lucas.

Hilde What do you mean? Of course you don't hate him.

Clara He's big and ugly.
  And he has a thing.

  Beat.

Hilde What thing, dear?

Clara His thing. He showed it to me.

It's shiny.
  And it sticks up like a rod.

  Hilde stares.

SCENE FIVE

Saturday. The Men of the Lodge, after the hunt. The drinking in the lodge. Lucas is there. Gunner. Theo. They are singing the drinking songs. Guns in evidence.

Song
  Will Rune Rune Rune drink a beer?
  Will he drink a beer?
  Oh will he drink a beer?

  Rune, a big man, downs a beer in one.

  For sure he will. For sure he will.
  Sure he will sure he will he will drink a beer!

  Will Theo Theo Theo drink a beer?
  Will he drink a beer?
  Oh will he drink a beer?

  Theo downs a beer in one.

  For sure he will. For sure he will.
  Sure he will sure he will he will drink a beer!

Later: Theo and Lucas. Tomas, Palme, Ragnar,
Gunner and Rune. Maybe others. Lively except for
Rune, who is asleep.

Theo Picture the scene. There are no women left on earth. None at all. Just men and beasts.

Gunner My God.

Theo I know. A bleak scenario. My question to you is this. Bestiality? Or celibacy? Which would you choose?

Tomas You mean fucking animals?

Theo Yes, Tomas, that's exactly what I mean.

Gunner What animal?

Theo A deer.

Gunner Why a deer?

Theo They're readily available. And they have a beautiful smooth arse. Come on, my friends. Make your decision. Would you deny yourself all pleasure, or go out there in the forest giving it to one to our antlered friends? Tomas? Gunner? Lucas?

Lucas How come there are no women on earth?

Theo That's not the point.

Lucas But how are we here, if there are no women?

Theo Jesus you can be a real pain in the arse. It's a game, Lucas. We're playing a game.

Lucas I'm just trying to understand the context.

Theo They all died in childbirth, all right?

Lucas All of them?

Theo Yes all of them. Except one who got run over by your pedantry. Answer the question. Would you fuck a deer?

Lucas Well, in that situation. I imagine we'd probably all end up fucking deer.

Beat.

Theo I thought so. Lucas is in fact a deer-fucker.

Lucas Oh I see . . .

Theo Sorry to tell you this everyone. It's what we feared.

He starts to sing.

Will Lucas Lucas Lucas fuck a deer?
Will he fuck a deer?
Oh will he fuck a deer?

Theo / Gunner *etc.*
For sure he will. For sure he will.
Sure he will sure he will he will fuck a deer!

Gunner Official confirmation. Lucas is a deer-fucker!

Theo Don't deny it, my friend. We've always known. The way you point that gun . . .

Lucas Theo, you are the biggest . . .

He chases Theo. Theo dodges. Chaos.

Theo / Gunner *etc.*
For sure he will. For sure he will.
Sure he will sure he will he will fuck a deer!

Rune wakes.

Rune Oy. Keep the noise down.

Theo Rune, we have a really important question.

Rune I'm trying to sleep!

Theo So. There are no women on earth. They've all died of a terrible disease. My question is –

Lucas's phone rings.

Gunner No phones in the lodge!

But Lucas is looking at his phone.

Theo Who is it?

Lucas Susanna.

Theo Don't answer it.

Lucas Why is she calling me at two in the morning?

Theo To ruin your evening. Lucas. Let it go to answer-phone.

Lucas Marcus could be in trouble again.

Theo Lucas, do not answer it!

Lucas answers.

Lucas Hello. Yeah this is me. No I'm at home.

Rune talks to Theo.

Rune What's the fucking question?

Lucas shooshes him.

It's just the TV. Susanna, calm down. What's happened?
Did he say that?
I did tell you. He wants to see me more.
Of course I would.
Sure. That would be great. Let's talk about it in the morning, OK?

He hangs up. Stands still.

Theo What did she say?

Lucas She said Marcus can come and live with me. It's what he wants, apparently.

Theo When?

Lucas Now. She'll come and drop him later this week.

Lucas smiles.

Theo That's good.

Lucas It is.

Theo That is really good, my friend.

They hug. Beat.

Just one thing. Does Marcus know you fuck deer?

Lucas Yeah, he knows.

Theo Cos I'd hate to be the one to break it to him.

Gunner turns to Rune.

Gunner Rune. The question is. No women on earth. And the deer are dead too. Would you fuck the Little Mermaid?

SCENE SIX

Clara stands there.
The schoolroom.
The clock says Monday 18 November. 8.32 a.m.
Clara and Hilde. Per, a member of the board, is there too. He has a laptop out.

Hilde Clara. Come in. Sit down. Clara, this is Mr Simenson from the board of trustees. He is our designated officer who deals with situations like this.

Per Hello, Clara. You can call me Per if you like.

Beat.

Hilde Clara, I need you to tell Per what happened on Friday after school. Can you do that?

Clara Tell him what?

Hilde Just tell him what you told me. About what happened with Lucas.

Beat.

Per Hilde said that on Friday you stayed in here with Lucas waiting for your mummy and daddy. And then. Something happened.

Hilde Remember what you told me . . . What did you say, darling?

Per Can you tell me what you told Mrs Gunnersen? Can you tell me what happened?

Clara I can't remember.

Beat.

Per Clara, it's hard for you, I know. To repeat it. But can you try?

Clara I can't remember.

Hilde You said to me that you didn't like Lucas any more. Do you remember saying that?

She shakes her head.

Per Clara. It's fine. Nothing is going to happen to you. No one is going to be angry. Just tell me what you told Mrs Gunnersen.

Clara . . .

Per On Friday afternoon. You were in this room with Lucas. Waiting for your mummy. Yes?

She nods.

Where were you? Were you where you are now?

She nods.

Good. Very good. And Lucas was where I am. Or where Mrs Gunnersen is?

She nods.

Where I am? OK, good.
And then what happened?

Beat.

Did Lucas give you this?

Per holds up the heart-shaped lollipop. Clara nods.

This lollipop? He offered it to you? And you refused it?

Clara nods. He types.

And then what happened?
Did Lucas show you something? Something he shouldn't show you?

Beat.

Hilde Clara, you can tell Mr Simenson.

Per What did he show you, Clara?

Clara Nothing.

Per So is Mrs Gunnersen making it up? What you said?

Clara shakes her head.

Or . . . were you making it up?

She shakes her head. Children's screams and laughter from the playground.

So. What did he show you?

Clara I want to go and play.

Per You will in a minute. When you've told us what happened.

Hilde Just say what you said to me, Clara darling.

Per And then you can go and play.

Beat.

Clara He showed me his thing.

Per He showed you his thing. His private thing. Yes?

Clara (Yes.)

Per Here in the classroom.

Clara (Yes.)

He taps on the keyboard.

Hilde And it was . . . you said it was . . .

Per What was it like, Clara?

Beat.

What was it like?
Was it shiny?

She nods. He taps on the keyboard.

And was it pointing up?

Beat.

Like a rod?

Clara nods.

Did he ask you to touch it?

Hilde Per. I never said. She never said.

Per Did he, Clara?

Long pause. She nods.
Hilde gets up, is nearly sick in the wastepaper bin.

Let's leave it there, Clara. Why don't you go back to Mrs Gunnersen's office for a drink. And then you can go and play.

Hilde I'll take you, Clara.

She gets up and leaves with Clara and the bin. Per sits in shock. Hilde returns. She looks very distressed.

Per The parents know nothing?

Hilde I didn't want to say anything until we were sure.

Per And Lucas is at home?

Hilde I left him a phone message. Told him not to come in.

Per I'll call him later, let him know his rights, give him some numbers he can call for advice. You didn't tell him the exact nature of the allegations?

Hilde On an answerphone message?

Per Did you say who was involved?

Hilde No.

She breaks up.

Per Have you ever suspected Lucas of anything like this?

Hilde No, of course not.

Per Any untoward behaviour?

Hilde He's only been here a term. But he's been terrific with the kids. You saw the harvest festival.

Per And the girl?

Hilde Clara has a vivid imagination. But about something like that? How would she even think of it?

Per Lucas lives alone, doesn't he?

Hilde Since his separation. Yes.

Per And how long has that been?

Hilde About a year.

Per Keeps himself to himself?

Hilde I suppose so. Why?

Per Just background information.

Hilde's phone rings. She answers.

Hilde Yes, Julie?
But I told him not to come in.

She puts the phone down.

It's Lucas. He's here. Oh Per, what do we do?

Per I thought you called him?

Hilde I did. I swear I did.

Enter Lucas. A spring in his step.

Lucas Morning.

Hilde Lucas . . .

Lucas Hello. Per.

Per Hello. Lucas.

Lucas How was the date?

Hilde The what?

Lucas The coffee date with the man of mystery?
We had a lively evening on Saturday. I ended up
having to carry Theo to his doorstep like a bride.
Where's the register?

He can't find it.

Hilde Lucas, didn't you get my message?

Lucas The hunting was hopeless. No one shot a thing,
it's like the deer knew we were coming. And then on
Sunday morning I wake up and I see this incredible doe

just yards from my window. What message?

Hilde On your phone?

Beat. He looks at his phone.

Lucas No. I must have missed it. You want me to listen to it, or can we do this live?

Beat.

Are you all right, Hilde?

Per You need to go home, Lucas.

Lucas What do you mean?

Per I will call you later and explain. But you need to go home now.

Lucas Per, what are you doing here?

Per I'm the member of the board with responsibility in this area.

Beat.

A child came to us this morning. They informed us that an inappropriate act took place last week. Here. At the infants' school. And that the inappropriate act involved you.

Hilde That's why I tried to call you. To stop you coming in.

Beat.

Lucas What act?

Per We prefer not to say. At this stage.

Lucas Can you say which child?

Per Not at this stage.

Beat.

It's necessary at this stage that you are not aware of the allegations made against you. There is a process that needs to be undertaken. We will need to suspend you, on full pay of course, while that process takes place.

Hilde The best thing, Lucas, is for you to take the rest of the week off.

Lucas Process?

Per There'll need to be some sort of investigation.

Lucas No, whatever it is, I'm sure we can sort it out internally.

Per I'm afraid that's impossible.

Lucas Maybe I can talk to the child. There must have been some kind of misunderstanding.

Per The allegation was made in strict confidence by a minor. The protection of the minor is therefore our first priority. We make no assumptions of guilt and will refrain from doing so until the investigation is complete. But as the allegation is not just one of professional misconduct but involves a potential crime, I'm afraid we must inform the police and local child welfare officers.

Lucas Per, if you do that, everyone will know. You know this town. People talk to each other.

Per Lucas, this is my area. You must trust me to deal with it.

Lucas Per, with respect, you are an accountant.

Per Nonetheless I am trained in this area.

Lucas What crime? What crime am I accused of?

Hilde Go home, Lucas. And talk to no one. For your own sake.

Lucas What about my class? They're expecting me.

Hilde We'll manage. Lotte's coming in for the staff meeting, I'll see if she can stay.

Per My friend. If you're seen to be obstructing the investigation . . . I just mean that if you appear to be making things difficult, it won't be helpful for you. The best thing you can do is go home. No judgement is being made on you at this stage. Full confidence will be observed. You have my word.

Lucas makes for the door. Then:

Lucas Was it Clara Kallstrom?

Hilde Lucas, please.

Lucas Was it Clara?

Per As I have already said, we cannot discuss any details of the allegation at this time.

Lucas It was Clara. Wasn't it?

Per Why do you make this assumption?

Lucas Just let me talk to her. I know both parents. Theo is my friend. It's a misunderstanding, it can be sorted out.

Per I can't let the child near you.

Beat.

Lucas, I'm going to call the police now. If you're still here when they arrive, that could be seen as a refusal to co-operate with the investigation. I cannot speak as to the consequences.

Beat.

Go home.

Lucas walks to the door. Turns to Hilde.

34

Lucas Hilde. Do you believe her?

Beat.
Blackout.

SCENE SEVEN

A Man from the Lodge, Rune, sings beautifully as he clips his hedge.

Rune
This is our country
Our country we love
We'll greet every enemy
With the sword in our hand.
To he who brings war
Through fields and on beaches
We will light bonfires
On our forefathers' graves.

He sees Lucas, who is walking.

Lucas Hi, Rune.

Rune You going home, Lucas?

Lucas Yes. Thought I'd take the forest path.

Rune Yeah, you should go home.

He sings.

Each town has its witch
Each parish its troll
We will with pleasure
Take the life from their veins
Yes we will with pleasure
Rip the life from their veins.

Lucas stares at Rune and walks on.

35

23 November. 6.35 p.m.
  Night. Lucas, tired from sleepless nights, sits on a
bench at the side of the road in a coat. The dog Max is
with him. He checks his watch. Peter enters.

Peter Hi, Lucas.

Lucas Hey, Peter. What are you doing here?

Peter I'm waiting for Dad. He told me to wait in the car
and I can keep the heating on and listen to whatever
music I want until he gets back. (*The dog.*) What's his
name?

Lucas He's called Max.

Peter He's big.

Lucas Is your dad at the meeting in the school?

Peter Yes, that's why the lights are on even though it's
night.

Lucas Do you know why they're meeting?

Peter No. I just know something's wrong because Hilde
looks really pale now all the time. Billy says she's dying
of a disease. Why aren't you at school any more?

Lucas I needed some time off.

Peter So are you coming back soon?

Lucas I hope so.

Peter Lotte's such a boring teacher.

Lucas Lotte's lovely.

Peter No, she's boring. She doesn't do fights or anything.
She just does adding up and being kind. Why are you
sitting here?

Lucas I'm waiting for someone to come out of the meeting. I need to talk to them.

Peter If you want to talk to them why don't you go into the meeting?

Lucas No, I'll wait. You should go back to the car and stay warm.

Peter The car's boring. There's biscuits in the meeting. But children aren't allowed.

He takes out his phone. Plays a game on it.

Lucas That's a nice phone.

Peter It was Dad's but then he got a new one so. It can do everything.

Lucas What are you playing?

Peter Medieval Evil. You have to climb the wall and avoid the barrels of boiling oil and the arrows and save the maiden. She's calling out for help in the tower.

Lucas Who's that other knight?

Peter That's another gamer. It's a race between me and him. He's in Korea.

Lucas I think he got there first.

Peter Yes. He did.

Noises from the school. They look up.

Someone's coming out now.

Lucas You should go back to your car, Peter.

Peter But Max is so warm. Aren't you, Max?

Lucas No, you should go now.

Peter I don't want to go home. Mum will be asleep, she's sick again. And Dad just watches TV on his own in the basement. It's too quiet.

Lucas What's wrong?

Peter I hate my home.

Beat. Lucas stares at him.
Enter Theo and Mikala in coats.

Theo Peter, what are you doing here?

Peter I was waiting in Dad's car. But then I saw Lucas and Max so I came to say hello.

Mikala Go back to your dad's car.

Theo Go back now, Peter.

Peter Why?

Theo Just do as you're told.

Peter Why?

Mikala Just do as you're told, Peter.

Peter Lucas, can I take Max for a walk? I'll bring him back. He wants a walk, don't you, Max?

Lucas Just bring him back.

Peter Come on Max. Let's go!

Peter leaves with the dog.

Mikala What are you doing here?

Lucas Didn't you get my messages?

Mikala We got them.

Lucas I didn't want to call at the house.

Theo No, that wouldn't be a good idea.

Lucas Can we please talk about this? We can go somewhere if you're worried about other people.

Theo We left the meeting early – so the others won't be coming out for a while.

Beat.

Lucas What's happening in there?

Theo Don't you know?

Lucas They don't tell me anything.

Theo Well, you know those school meetings. Hilde talks a lot. The red wine remains the worst I have ever tasted.

Lucas What did Hilde say?

Theo Nothing we didn't know already. The investigation is developing. They gave out pamphlets to help people understand. Ragnar's wife started to have a little cry.

Lucas Did they mention my name?

Theo At the moment they're just saying the incident involves a male member of staff.

Lucas I am the only male member of staff.

Theo There's Jan the gardener.

Lucas He's seventy.

Theo Maybe there's life in the old dog yet.

Mikala Theo, let's go.

Lucas Let me talk to Clara. Please.

Mikala Theo, I want to go home.

Lucas Something happened on that Friday . . .

Mikala Yes, we know. We know exactly what happened.

Lucas No, you don't. Before you came. Clara gave me

a present. A heart-shaped lollipop. She'd wrapped it specially, I refused it.

Mikala That's not true. You gave the lollipop to her.

Lucas Did she say that?

Mikala Are you saying my daughter's a liar?

Theo The lollipop was what they call your entry point. And then when she refused it, you smiled at her.

Beat.

You opened your trousers.

Mikala Theo.

Theo You took her hand. And you . . .

He is almost sick.

Mikala Theo.

Theo I need to say it.
You put my daughter's hand on your cock.

Beat.

Lucas Is that what she said?

Mikala That's what you did.

Theo gasps, can't breathe . . .

Theo? Are you OK?

Theo Can't breathe.

Mikala Sit down.

Theo I don't want to sit down!

He breathes deep.

Lucas Mikala, listen to me. You are my oldest friends. I love Clara. I've known her since she was a little baby. I would never . . .

Mikala Don't say it. Don't even say it.

Theo Where do they get that fucking wine?

Mikala Let's go.

Theo It's eating into my mouth.

Lucas Just let me talk to her.

Mikala Can you walk, baby?

Lucas Listen to me. It makes no sense. Even if I had wanted to do that, which I didn't, you think I would choose there? You could have arrived at any time. Why would I do that?

Mikala Maybe you enjoy the risk. I don't know what it's like to have such urges.

Lucas Let me talk to her. Not at the house. Somewhere neutral. You can both be there. We can ask her. Together.

Mikala Lucas, listen to me. I will never let you near my little girl again. Never. Ever. Again. You hear?

Lucas Someone from the town telephoned my ex-wife last night. They told her I was accused of touching Clara. They told her I was a risk to my son.

She's not letting Marcus come here any more.

He was going to live with me. Now he can't even see me.

Help me.

Theo Oh, Lucas. Lucas.

Theo suddenly grabs Lucas. Is it a hug? No, he starts to squeeze him hard.

My girl. My little girl.

Mikala Theo. Theo, stop.

They struggle. Theo moans. Then he throws Lucas off. Beat.

Theo Oh, I should say. Something else happened at the meeting.

Mikala Theo, we're not supposed to tell anyone that.

Theo It's why we left early, come to mention it.
At the meeting, Lucas, we were told that another child has come forward.

Lucas What do you mean?

Theo Another of your victims. Has come forward.

Theo and Mikala stare at Lucas.
Blackout.

Interval.

Act Two

SCENE ONE

The infants' school.
18 December. 9.45 a.m.

Hilde The aim of asking you here is to give you an
update on the investigation and tell you how we will
proceed from here.

I'm afraid to say that three other children, whose
names will remain anonymous, have now come forward.

Lucas Bruun has been suspended from post without
notice and has been served with a police restriction order
banning him from coming within half a kilometre of the
school or any of the children.

I know. Of course. I am aware. What is in all your
minds. It seems we may have a case of repeated abuse in
our school. We take this allegation very seriously. But we
must let the police do their work.

When we first told you about this, we asked you to
keep an eye on your own children and to observe any . . .
symptoms that were in anyway unusual. Bed-wetting.
Headaches. Nightmares. That sort of thing.

If they haven't already, the police will come and ask
you questions. About your child. Or children. They will
also need to talk to your child as they pursue their
enquiries prior to a possible charge.

We are just a week away from the festive holidays. We
will continue with the carols and the Nativity. Christmas
is a time for the children. It must stay that way.

This is our community. Whatever has happened must
not defeat us.

Does anyone have any questions?

Blackout.

Theo and Mikala's house. Clara is sitting cutting out
Christmas paper decorations. Cutting a pile of paper
angels that then fold out.

Mikala There, Clara. Cut it there. Mind his head.

Clara How many are we making?

Mikala As many as you want. OK?

Clara They're pretty.

They fold them out and look at the angels.

Mikala When Daddy gets back we'll hang them up, shall
we?

Clara Is Lucas coming at Christmas?

Mikala Not this year, no.

Clara But he always comes.

Mikala I don't think he's coming this year.

Clara Can I go and walk Max?

Mikala Why do you want to walk Max?

Clara I like walking him.

Mikala You can't, darling. Not at the moment.

Clara Is it because of what I said? I just said something
silly. And now all the children are talking.

Mikala Clara. I know this is hard. But we can't pretend
something didn't happen just because we want everything
to stay the same. OK? Something happened. And now
we have to move on.
      Let's do some more. Cut there. That's it.

I'm going to spend more time at home with you, all right? I know things have been a little crazy. We're going to solve that. Would you like that?

Clara nods.

Then that's what we'll do. You and me. OK?

Clara OK.

Theo enters.

Theo Hi.

Mikala You're back early.

Theo Hey, Clara. These are beautiful.

Clara We're going to hang them by the tree.

Mikala How was your day?

Theo Good. I dropped by the store on the way home. I got a remote-control plane for Torsten. What do you think?

Mikala I think he'll like it. How much was it?

Theo Does it matter? (*He spots an angel with one wing.*) Hey, look. What happened to this one?

Clara I cut one wing off with the scissors. But Mummy said it's OK anyway.

Theo Of course it's OK. It just means it can only turn in one direction. Like this.

He turns on the spot like a one-winged angel. Clara laughs and copies him. He hugs her.

You're my angel. You know that.

She nods.

Listen. I need to talk to your mother. Go upstairs to your brothers for a moment.

Clara But we need to finish the decorations.

Theo You'll finish later. Go and make a list for Santa, OK? Ask Torsten to help you. Make sure you don't forget anything because Father Christmas is very precise when it comes to lists and he has to organise his sleigh very carefully. I'll call you when we're finished.

Clara I want a dog.

Theo Well, write it down. You never know.

She leaves.

Now we have to get her a dog.

Mikala Maybe we should. She'd like that.

Theo And who'd have to walk it every morning?

Mikala Might make you get up.

Theo Yeah, it might.

Beat.

Mikala Are you OK?

Theo Lucas has been arrested.
The police came to his house this morning.

Mikala Who told you?

Theo I saw Gunner in the store. Apparently Astrid was walking in the woods and saw him being put in an unmarked car.

Mikala What happens now?

Theo They have three days before they have to charge him or let him go.

Mikala So he could be inside the police station for Christmas?
What about his dog?

Theo What about it?

Mikala What happens to it?

Theo Why are you thinking about his dog?

Mikala Clara was saying she wanted to walk it.

Theo Did you encourage her?

Mikala No, of course not.

Beat.

Theo What's wrong?

Mikala Why did Clara like him so much? Why did she feel the need to seek him out?

Theo She didn't feel the need. He groomed her like he groomed the others.

Mikala But she always liked him, Theo. Felt comfortable with him. More than with us.

Theo This has nothing to do with you and me.

Mikala Wasn't there something we could have done? To be closer to her.

Theo Stop it. It doesn't help.

Mikala Did you ever suspect he could do such a thing?

Theo Never. But maybe I never knew him. All those years. Coming to this house. Quietly eating our food. Maybe he was just offering a version of himself.

Mikala Do you ever do that to me? Offer me a version?

Theo Of course not.

Mikala I do. Sometimes. To you. Maybe that's all any of us do. Maybe we're all just strangers.

Theo Mikala. Look at me. I am not a stranger. Not to you.

Mikala You should tell Clara. That he's been arrested.

Theo Does she have to know?

Mikala She'll find out from the other children anyway. It's better she hears it from you.

Theo You want to come with me?

Mikala You do it. I'll make supper.

Theo leaves.
Mikala stands alone.

SCENE THREE

Christmas Eve. 7.45 p.m.
The Christmas Lodge drinks. The Men of the Lodge.
Dead deer hanging.

Song
Will Tomas Tomas Tomas drink a beer
Will he drink a beer
Oh will he drink a beer?

Tomas downs a beer.

Yes he will yes he will he will drink a beer.

Gunner Now the last time we were here, we shot nothing. Not one thing! Today we got a bounty!

Cheering.

It's a good omen, friends. A blessing from nature. This festive season will be the best yet. Theo would like to raise a toast!

Ragnar A toast, Theo!

All A toast!

Theo stands. He is sombre.

Theo I'd like to raise a toast to all of us. To this lodge. To my friends. To my community. In times good and bad. We are together. Thank you.

They raise a glass. They sing slowly, almost sombrely.

Will Theo Theo Theo drink a beer
Will he drink a beer?
Oh will he drink a beer?

Theo downs a beer.

For sure he will sure he will he will drink a beer!

Enter Lucas. His hair is longer, he is unshaven. Silence in the lodge.

Lucas Is there a beer for me?
    Hi, everyone. Hi, Gunner. Theo. Rune. Tomas. Ragnar. Palme. Happy Christmas.

Gunner How come you're out?

Lucas Oh . . . they weren't allowed to keep me any longer. They asked me a lot of questions. But apparently they didn't find enough evidence to charge me. Not yet anyway. So here I am. How was the hunting? Looks like it went OK.

Gunner I thought the children gave evidence . . .

Lucas Yes, they did. Four of them now. They all said the same thing. That I exposed myself to them at the school. And that I invited them to my house to play with my dog Max. That I made them undress. In my cellar . . . and touched them. The police searched the house. You know what they found?

Theo They found that you don't have a cellar.

Silence.

Lucas So now I'm free to go home. The school will still have its disciplinary hearing. And the police may choose to charge me at a later date should new evidence arise. That's the sum of it. Is this mine?

He sits. Reaches for a beer. It is taken from him.

Gunner You should go, Lucas. This isn't the right time.

Lucas I'll just have one beer. If that's OK.

He reaches for the beer. It is taken from him by Rune.

Gunner It's not OK.

Lucas I am a member of the lodge, Gunner. I've paid my dues.

Gunner You may not have a cellar. That's a detail. It changes nothing. Not for us.

Lucas I have a Christmas beer here every year.

He reaches for a beer. It is taken from him by Rune. He reaches again. It is taken from him. But he holds tight on to it. Beat.

Gunner Lucas, listen. It's better you don't come into town any more. You don't come to the lodge. You don't go to the store. You don't go to church. We don't want to see you until the hearing is done.

Lucas They didn't charge me. I am free to be here, according to the law.

Gunner You think we trust the law on these matters? You read the papers. They never charge anyone.

Lucas So what do you suggest we do?

Gunner What do I suggest?

Gunner smashes his fist into Lucas.

It's Christmas. We want to spend it with or families. Go home and stay inside. That's what I suggest.

Lucas takes the drink. Stands on the table. And drinks it. He begins to bang the table as he sings.

Lucas
Will Lucas Lucas Lucas drink a beer?
Oh will he drink a beer?
Will he drink a beer?
Lucas Lucas Lucas will he drink a beer
Will he drink a beer?
Oh will he drink a beer?

The Men of the lodge leave as Lucas downs his beer.

Yes he will yes he will he will drink a beer!

SCENE FOUR

Christmas Eve. 10.45 p.m. Lucas's house. Darkness inside. A figure in the darkness. Waiting.
Lucas enters his house through the woods. His dog greets him.

Lucas Max! Max! Hey boy. Yeah, it's me. Sorry I left you. You want to go out? Yeah I'll take you out.

He opens the back door. Lets the dog out.
 Senses something. Turns.
 Sees the figure in the dark in the house.
 Lucas grabs a hunting stick.

Who's there? Who the fuck is there?

A light turns on. It is Marcus. Sixteen years old. Staring scared.

Marcus It's me. It's just me.

Lucas Marcus. Shit . . .

Marcus I didn't mean to shock you.

Lucas What you doing with the lights off?

Marcus Didn't want you to be scared when you came back.

Lucas Well, that worked a treat, didn't it?

Marcus Max didn't even bark. He knew it was me. I spent the last hour hugging the idiot.

Lucas Why didn't you call me?

Marcus I have no credit on my phone.

Lucas Does your mother know you're here?

Marcus Sure. She dropped me off.

Lucas And she's OK with that?

Marcus I told her you'd been released. I'll go back to her after Boxing Day. She says hi.

Lucas You nearly scared me to death.

Marcus Sorry.

Lucas Come here.

They hug.

I'm sorry there's no tree or Christmas lights.

Marcus That's OK.

Lucas I don't have a present for you.

Marcus It's OK.

Lucas I've been preoccupied.

Marcus You've been in custody, Dad.

Lucas We'll get some holly from the woods tomorrow. Make a fire.

Marcus I'd like that.

Lucas You want a beer?

Marcus You've had one already. I can smell it.

Lucas Well. It's Christmas, isn't it?

Lucas opens the beers. He hands him one.

Marcus Never had beers with you before.

Lucas Well, it's about time. Cheers.

Marcus Cheers.

He drinks it fast.

Lucas Hey. Take it slow. OK?

Marcus smiles.

Marcus Where've you been tonight?

Lucas I went to the drinks earlier at the lodge. We used to go every year. Remember? Drinks at the lodge and then presents at home and then Christmas Eve Mass at the church. You always loved that.

Marcus And it was OK? You being there?

Lucas Did I tell you? Gunner wants to initiate you.

Marcus Oh yeah?

Lucas He's sure you'll be a crack shot.

Marcus I'm not like you. You're ice-cool. I get all nervous.

Lucas I'm not ice-cool.

Marcus You don't show so much. Not like me and Mum. She shows everything.

Lucas You can say that again.

Marcus Does Gunner still want me in the lodge? After all this.

Lucas Of course he does. He loves you. All the guys do.

Marcus Are they supporting you?

Beat.

Lucas Not many. Palme maybe.

Marcus Any others?

Lucas (No.) I still have the disciplinary hearing . I can lose my job. And other children could come forward. So it's probably best you don't show yourself in the town. OK?

Marcus Why did Clara say what she said?

Lucas I don't know, I'm not allowed to see her.

Marcus Let me go. To Theo's house. Let me talk to her. She likes me.

Lucas I don't want you to be part of it.

Marcus Theo's my godfather. He'll listen to me.

Lucas I think it's best you don't get involved.

There's a knock at the door.

Marcus Who's that?

Lucas Leave it.

Marcus It's eleven o'clock on Christmas Eve. Who is it?

Another knock. Lucas takes a stick, opens the front door. Mikala stands there.

Mikala Hi.

Lucas Shouldn't you be opening presents?

Mikala Can I come in? It's freezing out here.

They enter.

Hi, Marcus. I didn't know you were spending Christmas with Lucas.

Marcus Well, here I am.

Mikala Are you allowed to be here?

Marcus The police released him.

Mikala But the investigation isn't over.

Marcus I don't care.

Lucas He's just staying until Boxing Day. Susanna knows.

Mikala How is Susanna? How's the city?

Marcus It doesn't stink like round here.

Lucas Marcus, go to your room for a few minutes would you?

Marcus Why?

Lucas I won't be long.

Marcus walks out.

Mikala Quite the welcome party.

Lucas He's upset.

Mikala We're all upset.

Lucas Do you want coffee?

Mikala I can't be long.

Lucas Theo know you're here?

Mikala He's still at the lodge. They're having a meeting.
Why did you go there today? That was stupid.

Lucas The police released me. I am free to move as I
desire, so long as I don't go near the children.

She lights a cigarette.

How is Clara?

Mikala She's fine. She always likes Christmas. She gets
to see her cousins and you know how much she loves
presents . . .
   She's the reason I'm here actually.

Lucas What do you mean?

Beat.

Has she said something?
   Mikala?

Mikala She's not been herself recently. And then tonight.
We were wrapping everything up. She asked me if Santa
would still come this year. Whether he'd still visit her.
I said of course he would. Why wouldn't he? She said,
'Because I'm a bad person.' I said, 'Of course you're not
a bad person.' She said, 'No I am. I lie. I lied about
Lucas.'
   Thing is I don't know whether to believe her. She's
said that sort of thing before. She could be protecting
you. She knows what's been going on with the police.
She's always liked you, Lucas. That's what's so awful
about the whole thing. She had such faith in you.

Lucas So do you believe her?

Mikala Maybe there was a confusion. Maybe Clara saw you somewhere private, and she thought she saw something. Did she see you somewhere strange? In the toilet maybe? You're always helping the children in there. And then she got it mixed up in her head.

Lucas No.

Mikala Then how did she know about what she said you did? How could she even use the words she used? I asked the boys, they swear they never showed her any photographs, magazines, nothing.

Lucas And you believe them?

Mikala They would tell me.

Lucas Have you asked Theo?

Mikala Theo is Clara's father. Why would he show her that kind of stuff? He doesn't even have that kind of stuff.

Lucas You sure?

Mikala Yes, I'm sure.

Lucas No secrets between you.

Mikala What does that mean?

Lucas Where were you that Friday afternoon? You said you were at work but you weren't.

Mikala How dare you?

Lucas I'm just saying. None of us are open books.

Mikala You've never been one. Have you? Susanna said she never knew you. Even after fifteen years of marriage. A total fucking stranger. Look at you now. Standing there. Cold. Indifferent.

Lucas That's not. What I am.

Mikala Who are you, Lucas? Do any of us know? Maybe you've had strange feelings for a long time, strange desires you didn't understand, maybe if you live like that long enough, alone, with all that anger, at Susanna, at women, it all comes out. Twisted. On to a little girl. Maybe you were conflicted but these feelings kept coming . . . and she understood them better than you did, Clara's sensitive, she notices things. And that's why she's trying to protect you. Some strange conspiracy between you. She was happy when I said you were released. She smiled. Is she protecting you, Lucas? Is that the hold you have on her? Is that the control you have over my little girl?

Lucas Mikala, I think you should leave. This isn't helping either of us.

Mikala Did you do something to her? Tell me. Please. Why can't you just show me something? Show me something, Lucas.

Lucas You should go.

Beat. She stands. Marcus enters. Watches her.

Mikala You know why the lodge are meeting?

Lucas No.

Mikala It's about you. What to do. I'm giving you a chance to tell the truth before it's too late.

Beat.

Marcus, you'd be better off spending Christmas in one of our houses. You'll be safe and warm. There's a Christmas tree. Hot food.

Marcus I'm staying with my father.

Mikala Do you know who your father is?

Marcus Do you know who your daughter is?

Mikala reaches the door.

Mikala (*to Lucas*) If I find out you're lying to me. If you've touched her. When they've finished with you, I'll have my turn. I'll cut out your eyes with a knife. I'll rip your balls off and I'll stick them on a spike outside my house for all to see.

She leaves.
Lucas stares out of the window.

Marcus What did she mean about the lodge?

Lucas I don't know. Call Max and shut the back door. Pull the bolt.

Marcus Max! Max!

Lucas locks the windows.

He's not answering.

Lucas We'll get him later.

Marcus I don't want to get him later.

Lucas He'll come back. Just bolt the door.

He closes the curtains.

You shouldn't have come.

Marcus I'm not scared.

Lucas I'll call your mother. Get her to pick you up.

Marcus No, don't.

Beat.

Lucas She didn't drop you off, did she?

Marcus (No.)

Lucas Does she know you're here?

Marcus I left her a note.

Lucas Oh great, Marcus. That's all I need. She'll come up here. You'll get me in more trouble.

Marcus She won't come. She's with her new man. She spends all her time with him.

Lucas A new man?

Marcus Didn't you know?

Lucas Is it serious?

Marcus It's always serious for the five minutes it lasts. But this one. Maybe. He's rich. Lives most of the time in Paris.

Beat.

I don't want to go. I want to stay with you.

He seems upset suddenly.

Lucas What is it?

Beat.

What is it, Marcus?

Marcus The police came three days ago. To our flat.

Lucas Did they ask you questions?

Marcus Yes.

Lucas . . .

Marcus They asked . . .

Lucas . . .

Marcus They asked me if you'd ever . . .

Beat.

Lucas What did you say?

Marcus I told them to fuck off.
I overheard Mum telling this woman police officer that you weren't honest with her. That she didn't trust you. That you she didn't know what you were capable of.

Lucas . . .

Marcus Why did she fucking say that to them?

Lucas She's still angry with me.

Marcus Why? She fucking left you!

Lucas Your mother and I met when we were very young. We had dreams – like any couple. But they got messed up, and a lot of years were wasted. You look for someone to blame and there's only each other. The damage can be deep, Marcus. You understand?

A distant gunshot.

Marcus What was that?

Beat.

Lucas Just the Christmas fireworks. It's nearly midnight.

Marcus They'll be going to church soon. Fucking hypocrites.

*He opens his bag, brings out a present. Wrapped.
It can't help but remind Lucas of Clara's present.*

Well then. Happy Christmas.

Lucas Oh, Marcus.

Marcus Open it.

Lucas hesitates, then opens it. It's a knife.

Lucas It's beautiful.

Marcus I found this shop near where we live.

Lucas It must be expensive. How did you . . .?

Marcus I hustled.

Lucas Did you now?

Marcus Yeah.

Lucas City boy.

Marcus Yeah.

Beat.

Lucas I should have a present for you.

Marcus Dad. It's OK.

Lucas It's not OK.

He breaks up. Beat.

Marcus Listen. We'll have a great Christmas. We can go for walks and roast sweet chestnuts. You have some?

Lucas I have some frozen. And blueberries.

Marcus Blueberry pancakes! You have flour? Butter?

Lucas I think so.

Marcus I'll make them.

Lucas Won't be as good as mine.

Marcus They will too.

Lucas Yeah, they probably will.
Where is that bloody dog? Check the back would you?

Marcus goes out the back.

Marcus Max! Max!

Lucas opens the door.

Lucas Max!

He looks out the front. Then sees something.

Marcus (*offstage*) Max! Max!

A large lump in a plastic bin bag lies outside the door. Lucas opens the black plastic bin bag. Gags. Enter Marcus.

I can't find him.

Lucas We'll look later.

He closes the front door.

Marcus What is it?

Lucas Nothing.

Marcus Don't lie.

He goes to the front door.

Lucas Don't look, Marcus.

Marcus Why not?

Lucas Don't open the door.

Marcus walks past, opens the door. Stares at the dead dog. Rain begins to fall.
Blackout.

Christmas Eve Mass. Rain outside. Pastor Lundgren greets the congregation.

Pastor For we must remember. Mary and Joseph gave birth to their child not in a major city of wealth and repute, but in a small, rural town not unlike our own. A town where people work hard to put food on the table, where they pay taxes, where they love and protect their families. In that sense, we all live in Bethlehem. And in Bethlehem a miracle occurred to save us all from our sins – the birth of our Lord Jesus Christ. Let us stand for the third hymn in our midnight Mass led by the children of the Sunbeam Infants' School conducted by Hilde Gunnersen.

Theo, Mikala, Gunner, Ragnar, Tomas, Palme, Rune, Per – all stand. Music plays.
The children enter. Hilde leads them in. Clara among them.
They sing.

Children
It came upon a midnight clear
That glorious song of old,
From angels bending near the earth
To touch their harps of gold!
Peace on the earth, good will to men,
From Heaven's all gracious King!
The world in solemn stillness lay
To hear the angels sing.

Enter Lucas. Covered in rain. He holds the empty dog's lead and collar in his hand.
He is immediately noticed. He sits in an empty pew, stares at Theo and Mikala.

Still through the cloven skies they come,
With peaceful wings unfurled,
And still their heavenly music floats
Over all the weary world.

Lucas joins in the singing. Almost primal in his grunts of pain.

Above its sad and lowly plains,
They bend on hovering wing,
And ever o'er its Babel sounds
The blessèd angels sing.

The singing stops. Lucas continues to sing.

Lucas
Yet with the woes of sin and strife
The world has suffered long;
Beneath the angel strain have rolled
Two thousand years of wrong.
And man, at war with man, hears not
The love song which they bring
O hush the noise, ye men of strife
And hear the angels sing.

Clara steps forward. Lucas stands. He stares at her. Hilde gets in between.

Hilde Lucas, get away from the children. Leave now.

Lucas holds up the empty lead.

Get away from my children!

Marcus bursts in. Walks up to Clara.

Marcus Clara, why are you lying?

Theo Get away from her.

Marcus Clara, why are you lying about my father?

Palme Get back!

Mikala Clara, come to Mummy. Clara! Come to Mummy.

Gunner Lucas, get your son out of here.

Marcus What did you do to our dog?!

Per This is a house of God, Lucas. Get your son out of here.

Rune Lucas. Get the boy out of here. Or I will.

He approaches Marcus. He speaks very quietly but the intent is clear.

Lucas Don't you touch him.

Gunner Then get him out of here. Now.

Rune continues to face up to Lucas.

Ragnar Theo, get your daughter home.

But Theo is frozen.

Mikala Let's go, Clara.

Marcus Clara, look at me!

Mikala Lucas, stop him!

Rune (*to Lucas*) Get out of my way.

Lucas Get away from my son.

Rune Lucas, this is my last warning.

Marcus Clara! I want to talk to you! I just want to talk to her!

Lucas Marcus, stay where you are.

Clara tears herself away from Mikala.

Mikala Clara!

Marcus walks towards her.

Marcus (*to Clara*) Why are you lying? You bitch!

He spits at her. Theo rushes forward, Rune too. Rune hits Marcus.

Marcus dashes out of the church. Lucas runs after him as the music plays.

SCENE SIX

Lucas's house in the woods. Daytime, a few days later.
Lucas walks in, limping, soil on his face. Spade in his hand.
Lucas sits. Studies some legal papers.
It is quiet.
There is a knock at the door.
Lucas quietly takes the rifle. Opens the door.
Theo is at the door.

Theo Hi.

Lucas Hi.

Theo There's no one with me. Put the gun down. As I said on the phone. I'm here to talk.

Lucas Talk about what?

Theo Please. Let me in.

Beat. Lucas lets him in, shuts the door, keeps the gun.

Is Marcus here?

Lucas He went back. His mother picked him up.

Theo Is he hurt?

Lucas He may have broken a rib.

Theo Well. It's probably best.

He looks at the spade.

Lucas I just buried Max.

Theo I had nothing to do with that.

Lucas In the garden.

Theo I had nothing to do with it.

Lucas Marcus wanted to have the funeral on Christmas Day but I persuaded him it wasn't in the festive spirit.

Theo What about spitting at my daughter? Smashing the lodge windows? Was that in the festive spirit?

Lucas He was angry. I'll pay for the windows. If that's why you're here.

Theo Put the gun down, for God's sake.

Lucas does not put down the gun.

Just give me a few moments. Please.
     Is there a drink going?

Lucas I'm out.

Theo Christ it's like visiting Calvin himself.

Lucas What is it you want to say Theo?

Beat.

Theo We were at school together. Played on the same teams. Fancied the same girls. Fancied Mikala. Remember those pig tails? That little gap in her bottom teeth? And then when she got breasts. It was like they appeared overnight. Everyone wanted a taste.
     I remember how kind you were when I married her. I knew you liked her. I think she liked you too. Anyway, I got her.

Lucas You're welcome to her.

Theo Isn't that the truth? But when women hold a flame, it never dies.

Beat.

I know Mikala came here. On Christmas Eve. I know she tried to warn you.

You see, she doesn't believe it. Doesn't believe her own daughter. Isn't that something?

I think she's going to stand up for you. In the hearing.

Lucas puts down the gun.

I think she's going to say that Clara is lying.

Lucas I didn't ask her to do that.

Theo Maybe not. But it does present me with a problem.

You see I refuse to believe Clara could . . . could make something like that up. Of course, now, after all this time she doesn't know what she thinks. The other children are inventing all sorts of shit. The whole town is talking about her, she can't walk down the street without people staring. Her own mother is doubting her. And that doubt is eating into her brain. But back then. On the day. She knew.

So you must have done something. Maybe not to the others. Maybe not in a cellar here in this house. But you did something. Something to her.

I've . . . come with an offer.

Lucas What do you mean?

Theo I want you to confess. Admit you did wrong.

And in return we'll drop some of the charges.

We'll drop the charge about touching. We'll keep it to indecent exposure. It's a lesser charge. It would be a first offence. You'd lose your job, but you'd only get a warning.

Beat.

Lucas Does Mikala know about this?

Theo We've talked it through at the lodge.

Lucas What about the other parents?

Theo They're willing to do the same. There'd be no hearing, no record, no register. You could move away. Start again. And so could we.

Lucas Where would I go? This is my home.

Theo Find a new one.

   Beat.

Lucas What about Marcus? He'd know I confessed.

Theo Tell him it was a deal you made.

Lucas Why would he believe me?

Theo If you don't take this, we will go after you with everything we have. This is your chance. Take Marcus with you. Begin a new life.

   Beat.

Lucas No. Please thank the lodge for their offer. But I can't accept.

Theo I'm trying to help you here.

Lucas No, you're trying to avoid your wife publicly shaming your daughter. It's not the same thing.

Theo I didn't need to come here. I didn't need to offer you anything. You have brought chaos into my home, into my daughter's life. And I am holding out an olive branch. Now take it.

Lucas If there is a chaos in Clara's life, it's not me that brought it.

Theo What does that mean?

Lucas If your house is in disarray, it's nothing to do with me.

Theo My house is not in disarray. I didn't say my house was in disarray.

Lucas Your father was a drunkard. He laid hands on you. Not tender ones. You carry that inside you. You need too much affection. You overflow the borders. My father was a private man, he was only happy on the Arctic ships. I carry that. You lack boundaries, I have too many.

Theo This has nothing to do with me or my past.

Lucas Did you ever ask Clara why she can't walk on the lines?

Theo She's a kid. Kids believe that stuff.

Lucas Not like her. She's in search of safety. All the time. She feels you can't give it to her.

Theo How dare you?

Lucas For some reason Clara thought I could provide the safety she craved. Now I don't know where she saw an erect penis or how she found out about that. Maybe one your boys left the internet on, maybe you did . . .

Theo Fuck you, Lucas.

Lucas Clara came to me needing safety. Safety from you. That gift she offered me was a request. I didn't accept it. That was my flaw. I didn't love her the way she needed me to. That is the mistake I made. Not that I loved her too much or in the wrong way. But that I didn't love her enough.

Theo Is that what you're going to say? In the hearing?

Lucas Maybe I should. But you know what I won't tell them? What I won't tell Mikala. Or anyone? Clara kissed me like a lover in that classroom.

Theo That's a lie.

Lucas And the strange thing is, I felt her love. She's six years old and I felt it like she was a fully grown woman. I told her that was for mummies and daddies. I told her that was for people we really adore. But maybe I was wrong. Was I?

Theo You sick bastard.

Lucas Go home, Theo. Close the door behind you, would you?

Theo pauses. Turns to leave. Then takes the gun. Looks at it. Takes it.

What are you doing?

Theo opens the gun chamber.

Theo Remember when we were young? In my parents' house. They'd be having a dinner party, they'd invite your parents, and you were allowed to stay the night. We used to listen from upstairs. And then one night you said we should pull our pyjama trousers down and go down the stairs with our cocks out. As far as we'd dare.

Lucas So what?

Theo So we did. I went further than you, of course. Nearly got caught. You thought that was funny. So funny. And then afterwards you looked at my cock and said, yours is thicker. And you touched it. You remember that?

Lucas Yes, I remember. So what?

Theo Well it's a bit weird, isn't it?

Lucas No it's not. It's not weird. It's what kids do.

Theo Was it already beginning then? Those private thoughts? Behind that face like a blank page?

He loads the gun.

Lucas Come on. What are you doing?

Theo breathes. Senses the silence.

Theo I adore these woods. It's so quiet. No one for miles.

He stares at the gun.

Lucas Theo, Clara is young, something happened to her, some kind of shock to her system. There is a reason she said what she said but I am telling you the truth.

Theo It's just words.

Lucas I am your friend! Yes, I can be cold. I can be aloof. I did fuck everything up with Susanna. But I've suffered for it. I've lost my son as a result, I have lost the woman I loved more than anything. I could barely leave the house for two months after she left. I couldn't get out of bed. If you didn't notice I'm sorry. If you saw a blank page, fine. But I am not *that*.

Theo I loved you so much.

He almost hugs Lucas. He tries to stick the gun in Lucas's mouth. Lucas struggles.

Tell me the truth, friend. Is this how you wanted it to be?

Gets the gun in his mouth.

Is this where you wanted to put it, huh? Right in her mouth? Right here? How deep did you want to go? This deep? Huh? This deep? *How deep did you want it?*

Suddenly Theo's phone rings. Theo keeps the gun there a little longer but his phone rings again.
Theo slowly lowers the gun. The two men stare at each other as Theo brings out his phone.
He stares at the number. He answers.

Hi, love.

Mikala, slow down. I don't understand what you're saying.

Beat.

I said slow down. What about Gunner? What exactly did he say?

Beat.

He found what?
 What was that doing on Peter's phone?

Beat.

Are you sure? Are you sure he said he showed it to Clara?

Beat.

She said that? She said she saw it?

Beat.

Yes, we must.
 No, let me do it. I'll call him.

He is looking at Lucas.

Yeah, it's good news.
 It's over.

SCENE SEVEN

The lodge. The Men of the Lodge are there. Hilde. And Mikala. And the kids. Gunner is speaking.

Gunner Well now! The spring initiations. My favourite time of the year! When boys become men and men become boys! The bluebells are sprouting, the lodge has new windows (thanks to a certain young friend of ours!) and the songbirds are making their own sweet music in the trees. And this spring is a very special one indeed. A boy steps into manhood as winter fades. What better way?

This boy of course has been sixteen for a while. There was a minor delay. We thought we had lost him to the 'big smoke'. But now he's back. In our town. In our hearts. And in our hunt.

And if he's anything like his father, the deer have every reason to fear.

Marcus. Congratulations.

Lights up on Marcus, Lucas. Clean-shaven, smiling, suited. Theo is there, Mikala, Hilde. Per. All smiling.

Come and accept your prize! This gift has been in your family for many years. This is from your father.

He hands Marcus a package. Marcus opens it. It is a shotgun.

Gunner Say something.

Marcus Sorry about the windows.
No, I'd like to thank everyone for this special day.
It's lovely. I wish everyone a good hunt this afternoon.
And most of all I'd like to thank my dad. For the gun. For teaching me to shoot. And for everything.

Pause.

Gunner Well. Let's party!

SCENE EIGHT

The lodge. Clara and Lucas. On opposite sides of the room. Party going on.

Lucas Hi, Clara. How are you?

Clara I'm OK.

Lucas Are you having trouble crossing the room? Quite a lot of lines on the parquet floor. Yes?

Clara Yes.

Lucas Do you want me to help you?

Clara Yes, please.

He walks over. He gently takes her in his arms. He carries her. Over the lines.

Lucas There we are. That was all right, wasn't it?

Clara Thank you.

She kisses him, on the cheek.

Lucas You should find your parents now.

Clara How is Max?

Beat.

Lucas Max? Max is fine.

Clara Can I come and walk him one day?

Lucas Maybe.

He sees Mikala is watching them across the room.

Now you go and enjoy the party. OK?

Clara OK!

She leaves smiling. Lucas alone.

SCENE NINE

The forest. Lucas stands with Marcus.

Lucas Can you hear it? Due west.

Marcus Deer?

Lucas You circle round by the trees, I'll come from this side. Beat it towards you.

Marcus OK.

Lucas Don't miss.

Marcus And ruin the family name?

Beat.

Lucas Marcus.

Marcus Yes.

Lucas Nothing. Go.

Marcus leaves. Lucas stands in the forest.
He breathes. Smiles. Takes out a cigarette.
A figure, distant. Silhouette.

Marcus? Is that you?
Marcus?
Who is that?
Who are you?

A shot rings out. Grazes a tree right next to Lucas.
Lucas flattens himself against the tree. Breathing
hard.
The silhouette disappears.
Lucas stands alone.

End.